Piano Solo

Contemporary Christian Christmas Solos

ISBN 0-634-04751-5

HAL•LEONARD®
CORPORATION

7777 W. BLUEMOUND RD. P.O. BOX 13819 MILWAUKEE, WI 53213

Visit Hal Leonard Online at
www.halleonard.com

ALL IS WELL

Words and Music by MICHAEL W. SMITH
and WAYNE KIRKPATRICK

781.723 Co Christmas

Contemporary Christian
Christmas solos

4

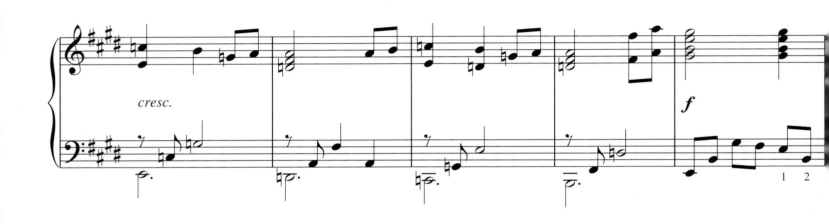

CELEBRATE THE CHILD

Words and Music by
MICHAEL CARD

THE CHRISTMAS SHOES

Words and Music by LEONARD AHLSTROM
and EDDIE CARSWELL

To Coda ⊕

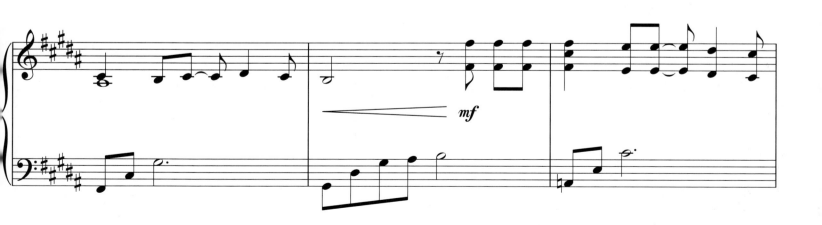

D.S. al Coda

CODA

EMMANUEL

Words and Music by
MICHAEL W. SMITH

Moderately fast

add light pedal

To Coda

GOING HOME FOR CHRISTMAS

Words and Music by STEVEN CURTIS CHAPMAN
and JAMES ISAAC ELLIOTT

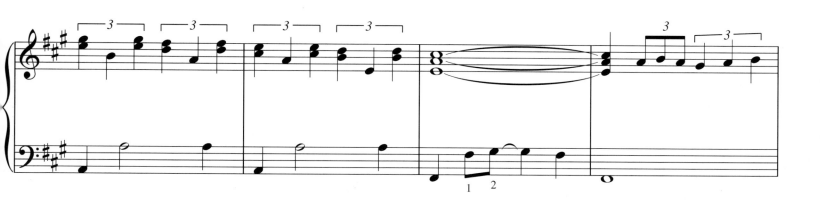

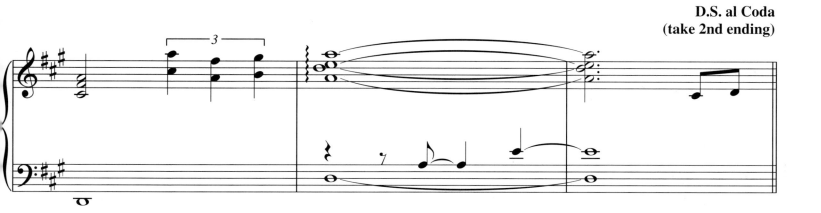

CODA

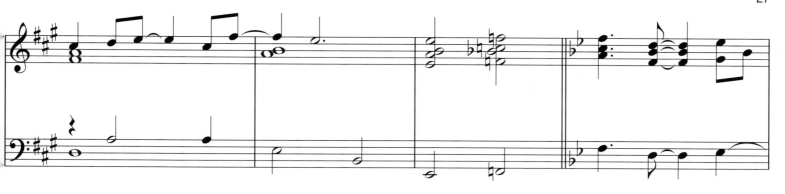

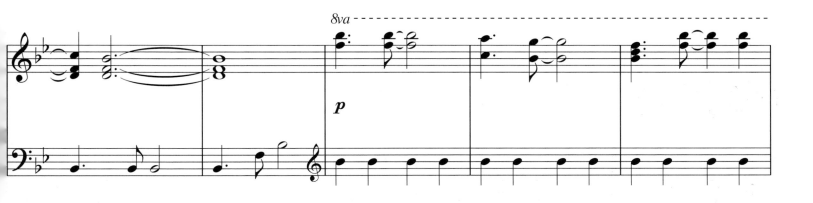

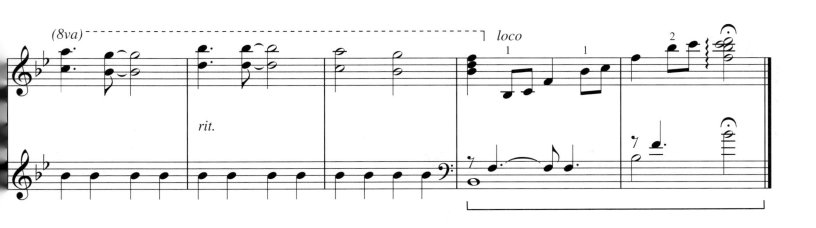

GOOD NEWS

Words and Music by
ROB MATHES

Moderately, with much expression

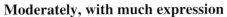

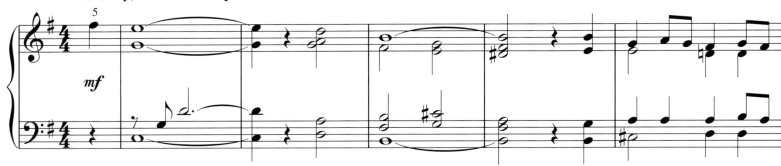

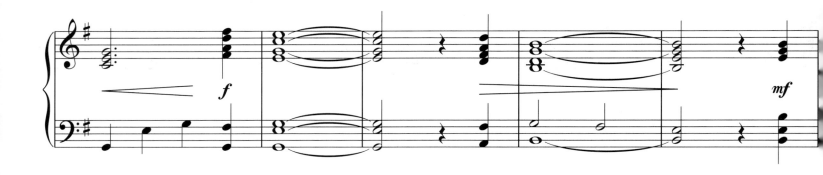

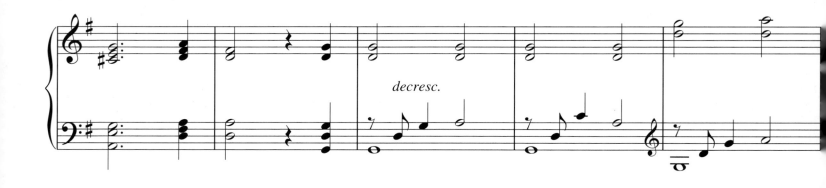

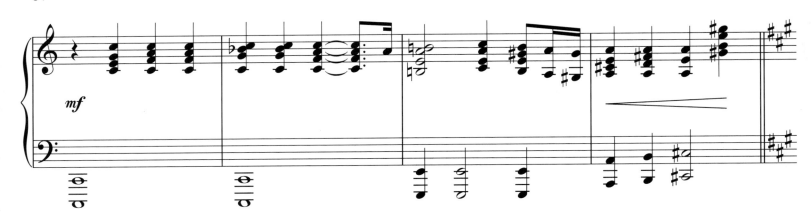

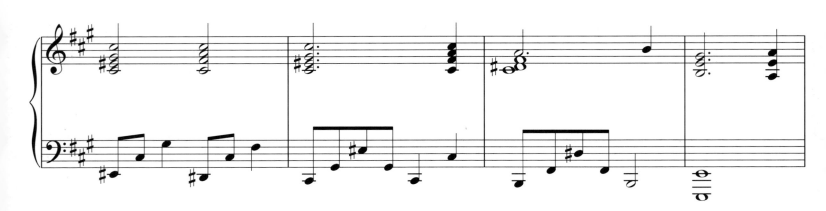

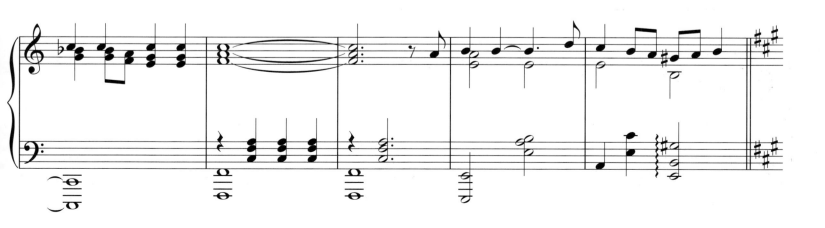

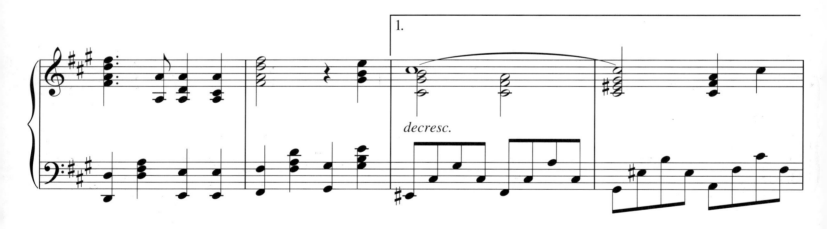

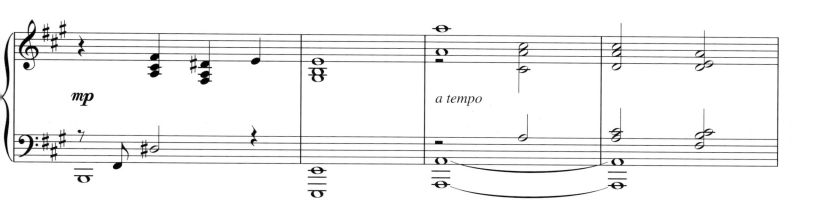

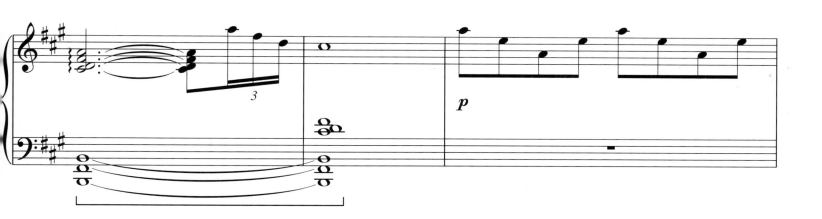

JESUS IS BORN

Words and Music by STEVE GREEN,
PHIL NAISH and COLLEEN GREEN

sub. *p*
bring out melody

mf

PRECIOUS PROMISE

Words and Music by
STEVEN CURTIS CHAPMAN

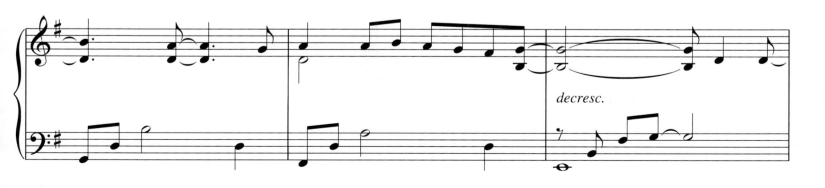

decresc.

To Coda

D.S. al Coda

CODA

THIS LITTLE CHILD

Words and Music by
SCOTT WESLEY BROWN

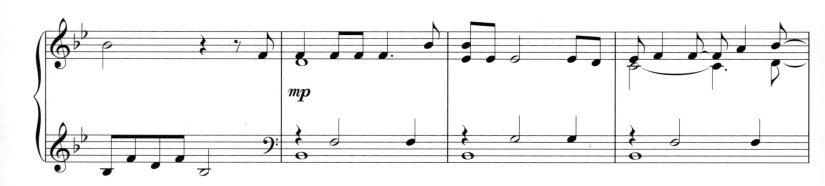

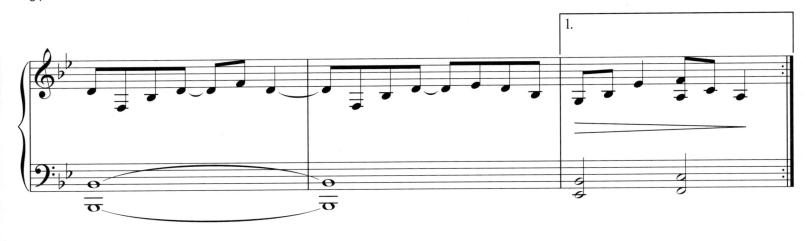

rit. e dim.

mp
a tempo

ROSE OF BETHLEHEM

Words and Music by
LOWELL ALEXANDER

THIS BABY

Words and Music by
STEVEN CURTIS CHAPMAN

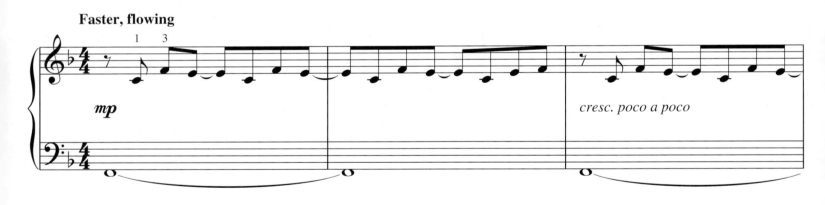

D.S. al Coda

CODA

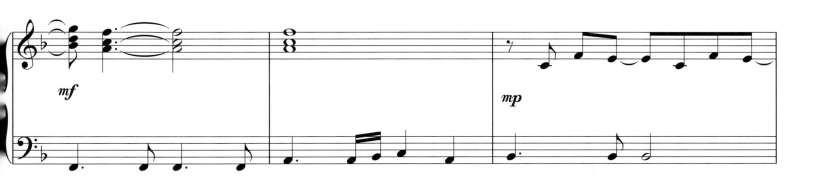

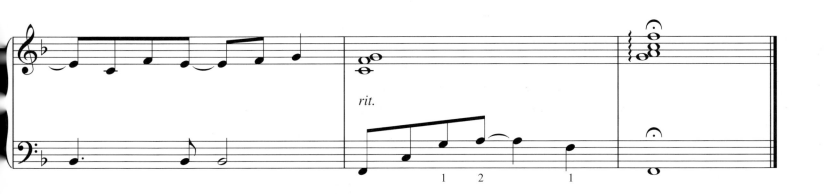

UNTO US
(Isaiah 9)

Words and Music by LARRY BRYANT
and LESA BRYANT

With energy

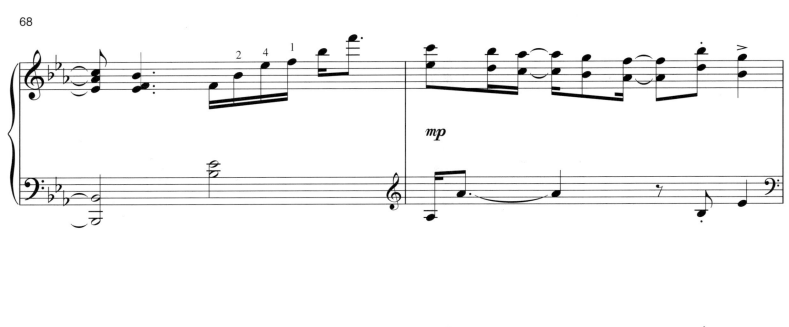

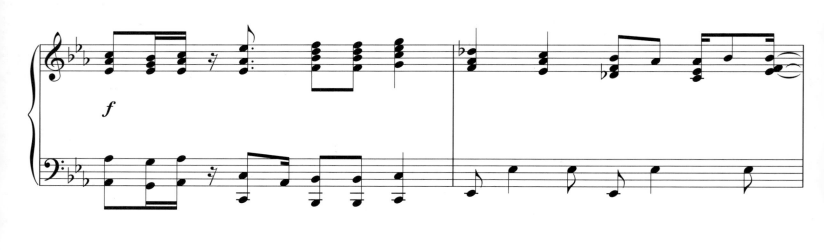